FLUX

FLUX

Orion Carloto

Andrews McMeel
PUBLISHING®

For
the ones who taught me how to be
a better lover and an even better writer.

My Dearest Reader,

Falling hopelessly in love is one magical adventure, but falling out is one seldom spoken. I've been in the type of love that sweeps you off your feet to the type of heartbreak that makes you feel as though you've lost a limb. But if there is anything that I've learned from each of them, it's that they're all different. Each and every heartbreak I've experienced so far in my life has come from different people, different situations, and a whole different kind of love. And, to me, that's the beauty of romance. Falling in all sorts of mad ways. That's where the birth of *Flux* came into play.

I wrote these words from my many states of grief, showing the good, the bad, and the ugly within my head. I wrote these words during the darkest pits of my depression, when the monsters were louder than my own consciousness. I wrote these words when the one thing I feared the most (change) was becoming my reality. I wrote these words with a flashlight, an inked pen, and an old Moleskine under my cotton duvet. I wrote these words for him, but he never appreciated them. I wrote these words for her, but I was too afraid to admit it. I wrote these words in hopes that they would heal.

I wrote these words for me, but now I want these words for you.

So here I am, one year on and deeply and madly in love with the woman whom I've become. And if perhaps I am a better person today than I was when I was hurt, it is because of them.

Flux is best read with a cup of warm coffee in hand.
Indulge in these words as if they were meant for you.

All of my love,

Orion. x

Flux, n.

The natural state. Our moods change. Our lives change. Our feelings for each other change. Our bearings change. The song changes. The air changes. The temperature of the shower changes.

Accept this. We must accept this.

—*The Lover's Dictionary,* David Levithan

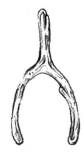

Sometimes things must break
in order for the wishes
we've longed for the most
to come true.

—we were inseparable lovers, both holding on tightly to the ends of wishbones.
it wasn't until you broke it off and ran away did i realize that, maybe,
this is exactly how it was supposed to happen.

May 8, 2016

Perhaps I'll just start off by saying that he left me. Like everything else in my life – nothing is forever, its all temporary. Its funny though because usually when someone leaves, there a reason, an alibi as to why forgetting is the best option – but he never gave that to me. One magical year was put to waste for reasons unknown. I knew from the moment I met him that something would hurt me, I just didn't expect it to come so soon. I fell deeply in love, down to my marrow. Things were different with him, nothing in this god damn world could ever compare. I suppose this was all just a fabricated time filler until something better comes along.. "I can't wait till I see your face and my brain thinks I'm looking at a stranger".

"you wrote 'don't forget' on your arm," Flatsound.

5

Crashing Cosmos

We met on an early autumn afternoon talking over earl grey and vanilla coffee. As if the gold and amber skies weren't enough to make me fall in love, the way your eyes crashed like cosmos in the night sky into mine certainly would do the trick. Defining a feeling like this is nearly impossible by words.

A moment I wish I could savor forever, capturing it raw and storing it in a tiny silver box on my bedside table. Luckily for me, I don't have to do that. Because this feeling is very much present,

every time you come around.

Delusional

Nostalgia clouded
in thoughts
for a love
that never
existed.

An Affair with Uninvited Feelings

We spent our summer
forgetting one another's
touch,

but as winter
rolled around,
we were only reminded
of the warmth we shared
in each other's arms.

Tainted

You asked me
to point out
exactly where
you hurt me,

yet
you had my hands
tied behind my back.

—things were unhealthy between us that summer; that's all i could remember.
i'm unable to trace back the times where you ever made me feel safe;
it's all just blurry to me now. without going into the painful
details of it all, let's just say that i learned to block out that time
in my life. your character was deceiving and it began reflecting.
it's been years since;
i hope you've changed.

Ghosted

Last night,
I was drunk
on your
words.

This morning,
I am hungover
on your
silence.

Flesh and Bone

His words cut the deepest wounds into my fragile flesh.
My vulnerability of attempting to clean up the blood was only
failed by missed calls and fits of unbearable confusion.
A sever far too deep, leaving my bones exposed
that not even a stitch could heal the wound.

He walked away with my questions left unanswered and a
consciousness filled to the brim with ache and insecurities.

If you asked him how he felt, he'd probably look away in fear
of exposing any emotion. A coward hidden beneath his layers too
afraid to convince, even himself, that it's okay to
mourn.

He was always 5 steps ahead of me,
dreaming of the next place he could be.
And while I tried running as fast
as I could to catch up,
hanging on to the little breath that I had,

I always stayed behind,
rag in hand,

cleaning up the blood.

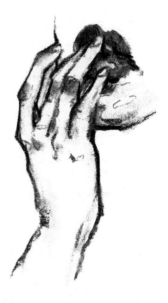

Daydreaming

I kissed him once,
for desire,
and, twice,
to forget.

Somehow,
I still tasted
you.

Gray Matter

I've gone mad.

It's been 26 days since you've said goodbye, yet you continue to lurk within every existing corner of my mind. I tried convincing myself that with each passing day it would become easier, but at no chance has it ever. It's been 26 days without hearing your voice; you haven't even called to check up. I've ripped at my hair, drove my palms deep into the sockets of my eyes, thrashed my temples
    over
    and over
    and over
    again
and you're still there.

Skin now embedded underneath the tips of my fingernails from digging into my cheeks just to get you out from underneath.

Day-old bruises resting soft upon my neck from the bones of my fingers attempting to grasp a better understanding as to why you thought this would help us.

I've howled at walls until my screams grew empty:

it's an unbearable loss,
an unknown despair.

What have you done to us, my dear?
What have
you done

to me?

you are a dream and i don't want to wake up.

Running

How dare you
have the confidence to say

    "I love you more"

when my weary vessel aches
from trying to run after you.

Character Development

Progress is dancing to the same song I used to cry to.

Your Girl

I crave to be the one you want,
photograph me in black and white.
Run your fingers through my hair,
tease me with a bite.

Tell me I'm your midnight muse,
write about me when you're alone.
Whisper to me all your secrets,
feel me in your bones.

Pick me up and read me,
like I'm your favorite book.
Reach inside my darkest thoughts,
until the very nook.

I wanted you beneath my arms,
the night you talked about committing,
I clenched my fists and begged to help,
but to you I wasn't fitting.

Moonlight

The left side of your bed will belong to
a girl with butterscotch hair.

The hands that used to wipe away my tears
will be the reason for her velvet moans.

The cologne I gifted you for your
birthday will smell like home to her.

The photographs you have of us will be deleted
to make room for her first time in New York City,
while I could barely fight the urge to take
the framed candid of us off my side table.

But while she's sleeping in your arms at midnight,
I hope you look out your window and remember
that my name will forever live in the stars.

And I hope you're reminded that no matter how hard
you close your eyes to try and forget the way I held you close,
you'll never escape the moonlight.

She

I read the promises you spoke
between your crooked teeth.

The gap between your
two fronts had more character
than the lines your smile
made permanent on your
caved-in cheeks.

You hissed scarlet rhythms
after each tap of your fingers
on the steering wheel.

Does she know your
breath smells of fresh
cigarettes only when
you've been drinking?

Does she know not to
talk about your father and
the brother that you miss
when you're feeling alone?

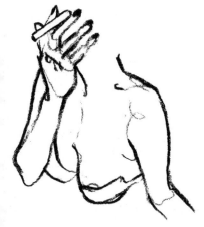

Does she know that
you have my words
tattooed on your wrist?

Did you tell her?

*"I knew I was addicted when it was 3 a.m.
and I was doing it by myself."*

Vultures

When I was a child, my mother once told me about the vultures and how they catch their prey. "Once a creature passes away, vultures and their keen sense of smell can detect a body from a mile away. They assemble together and fly in a continuous circle around the creature until it is decided to go in for the feasting." I've always thought it was strange that these wicked birds would create a ritual around a rotting carcass for minutes before perfecting the ideal time to devour. I think that's why it stuck with me all these years; they could sense death and that alone was fascinating to me.

When I was 19, the boy I loved decided to end things between us. An old tale of needing space in order to grow. For months, I could see the way he began carrying himself around me and I could almost predict what was bound to happen.

I just didn't fully believe it until my eyes traced 3 vultures flying in a circle over our heads when he was saying goodbye.

Loss

He set me up
for a loss
from the
beginning.

Letting a girl fall
for what
he knew
would
never
be.

Everything I wanted you to tell me:

"She isn't someone you have to worry about."

"Dwelling will only lead to overthinking."

"Your words are tattooed on my heart."

"I can't imagine a life without you."

"I'm sorry for making you cry."

"We will get through this."

"You deserve better."

"Come closer."

"I love you."

"I promise."

Chicago

I remember our nights in Chicago when I would follow you outside after dinner so you could smoke a cigarette. I didn't mind that it was 15 degrees out; as long as your presence was there to keep me warm, I'd follow you anywhere.

My arms wrapped around yours, we were rollicking in laughter under streetlights, our breath fading into smoke, dancing in the frosty January air. We were imagining what our lives would be like together. Growing up with each other in a tiny flat, just you and me, in the Windy City for years to come. Because saying we could just pick up our lives in Atlanta and move across the country was a lot easier said than done.

We began talking about how effortless our relationship has been. How we learned how to compromise—it almost felt as though our souls were attached from the beginning. That's what I tried convincing myself. You muttered under the warmth of your scarf, "It's been so easy for us; I'm afraid it will only get harder from here on." To which I reminded you, with a kiss on the cheek, that we could survive any passing storm that comes our way as long as we were hand in hand.

As our winter passed, and spring greeted us with blooming dandelions and stuffy noses, you left me.

You abandoned me in the storm alone. Without a hand to hold. Without any remorse. You left me on my hands and knees, screaming for answers.

You told me that things would only get harder from there on, so how did you make leaving me look so damn easy?

Haiku

Your love is like
a bittersweet haiku.

Kiss me five times,
lie to me seven,
apologize five more.

Repeat.

Thinking of You

I would
burn bridges
just to
hold your
hand.

"I'll Be Back"

He ran on false hope and empty promises.

Lake Michigan

A June spent by the lake, water saturated in color. Our bare feet
running carelessly across the warm sand as I chased after you for
a wet embrace. Layers upon layers of sunscreen on your freckled
cheeks, the pale on your shoulders already turning cherry as time
lingered. We climbed up towering dunes and swayed freely from rope
swings, capturing photos on film; I want this moment to live with me
forever. Our lips crashing together in unison with every wave, this is
how we spent our summer days.

A Coward's Lullaby

It's frightening because I learned more in your silence than I ever did in the time spent calling you mine.

Lucid Dreaming

I saw you in my dreams again; this time it felt more real than others.

Your hands were gripped tightly around my jaw,
or maybe it was just my covers.

don't get too close;
i'll turn you into
poetry.

Unforgettable

You'll think of me,
and regret what
you've done,
when you're
making love
to her.

PEACHTREE PLAZA

would it kill you to just put your pride aside for the slightest second
and ask me if i'm doing okay?

Mirror Talk

I was the only one watching myself fall apart;
    that's how I became the only one putting myself back together.

Indecisive

We hid our love
under inked skin
and sharpened teeth.

Tenderness revealing only
in our goodbyes,
for our hellos
would consist of
fingers crossed
behind backs and
bitten-down cheeks.

A wavering sense of hope
surrounding our bodies,
viridescent by nature,
that, perhaps, this time around
we were walking together,
blindly, in the same
meandering path.

Becoming immune to our
own indecisions,
there was not a doubt in my mind
that we'd fall right back to square one.

My baby doesn't believe me
when I tell him he can't live without me.
Because every time he tries to leave,
I always find him exactly where
I left him.

Russian Roulette

Your love was like a perpetual gun to my head.
With your fingers on the trigger
and a guessing game as to
which lie carried the bullet.

M

You still go by the same nickname
I gave to you.

The Birds and the Bees

We tiptoed on forest floors, skipping over pinecones and broken tree branches. Stumbling upon a honeysuckle shrub where we took turns savoring its sweet nectar. I'm allergic to the pollen that the season births, but at no point did that stop me from making love to you in a wild bed of red poppies that magical afternoon. We exchanged childlike giggles mid-kiss, smiles dancing recklessly across our faces.

Our love grew feverishly with the flowers that April.
An unforgettable swan song shared with the birds and the bees.

Bloody Knuckles

Day by day, I grow undone in his absence.

A fragile thing romance could be when flowers left on windowsills turn into muttered apologies under breaths. Slowly, I think I'm becoming quite lonesome again.

He stopped picking up my phone calls and I've begun scripting voice mails that are soon deleted. I'm on my third glass of wine and my train of thought is winding down a blurry track. I've now memorized his answering machine; I can recite it perfectly line by line. Do I feel proud or disturbed by this?

Call. Ring. Ring. Ring. Decline. *"Hey, you've reached my voice mail, can't get to the phone right now. Will get back to you soon!"* Please leave a message after the beep. Beep. Panic. Hang up.

Long after an aching farewell and biting down on knuckles until blood makes its way, I'm having trouble remembering the last time he told me he loved me and meant it.

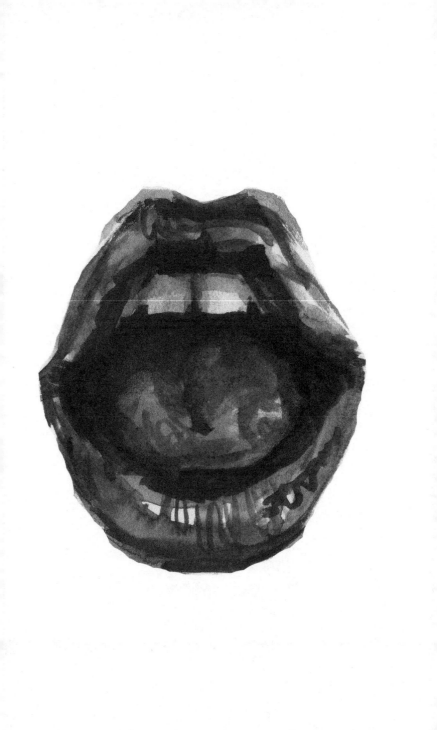

she was never sure of me,
but i was always certain of her.

Unrequited

To be in love
with someone
who is half in
love with you

is a game seldom
thought out and
prepared for.

*—that's high up on the list of
"things i never learned."*

Mixed Feelings

I couldn't tell you
what was worse.

When she went away
or when I realized
she wasn't coming back.

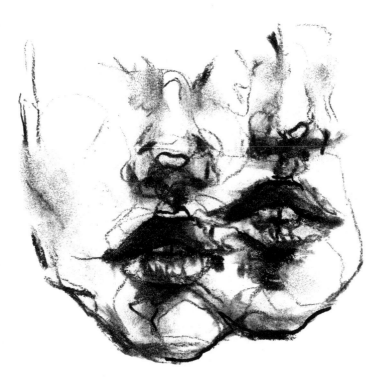

did i really love you if i didn't stop you from leaving?

Your Unsuitable Lover

Please don't fall in love with me.
I'll write about the way your collarbone curves into a perfect crater and how your bottom lip trembles when you're upset. I'll focus more on the way you twiddle your thumbs counterclockwise rather than the sweet nothings slipping from your mouth. I'll remember your favorite song until the lyrics are engraved into the crevasses of my skull, but I'll forget why you prefer coffee over tea. Please don't fall in love with me, because, once you realize that I'm not good enough, I'll write about you until my palms bleed and the bones in my fingers crack to serve as a reminder that I should have tried harder to make you stay. I should've focused more on the feeling you gave me when you held me close rather than counting how many goddamn freckles you have on your arms.

I should've woken you up to a fresh cup of coffee, not tea.

i'm afraid i'm not getting any better;

perhaps i'm getting worse with the seasons.

Hell

You
and
I
sin
divergently.

But
you
and
I
will
end
up
in
the
same
place
somehow.

Healing

Loss after love
is like a scab.

It will never heal
if you continue
to pick at it.

—all scabs turn into scars. and all scars have a story
to tell. so i guess you're kind of stuck with me forever.
(whether you like it or not.)

The First Time

I will savor your kiss
until our lips meet again.

Desire hung on our mouths
like a young boy clinging to
his mother's gown.

"you can't trust a coward,"

she said,

"but you sure can fall in love with one."

ROOM 1708

Finale

The moment of departure, confessing your final adieu, was the unforeseen instant that everything I ever knew passed away silently with grief.

The truth sounded bitter leaving your mouth—the wall that once separated us, built by an army of deception, was only growing in size and I could do absolutely nothing in my power to cease it.

As you walked me back to my car, we left a trail of unsaid affirmations and echoing sorrows behind us. To this day I could still hear the daunting voices in my head.

You didn't have to remind me that it'd be the last time I would hold your hand, when I already felt it in the way you hesitated to touch me.

—you wouldn't even kiss me goodbye.

March 28, 2016

I'm tired of trying to convince
myself that I'm okay. I'm not fucking
okay. Its been 20 days and nothing
has gotten better. They lied. They
said time will heal, but I'm only hurting
more with each and everyday that
passes and youre not mine. I keep
replaying the faint memory of you
saying goodbye over and over again.
Everytime I remember you saying those
words, a part of me dies inside. I
just want to know if you miss me. Do
you even think of me half as much as
I think of you? God I feel so sick. I
keep losing you over and over again
everytime I think of what we used to
be. I just want to know why you
walked out on us. I just want to
know what I couldve done to make
you STAY I've gone mad. I cant even
fucking think straight anymore. I cant
go to sleep without seeing you in my
dreams. I've dreamt so many times
that you want me back but I always
wake up in an empty bed. I just
wish I would have known when the last
time was going to be the last time.
I would've kissed you longer, held on
tighter, I would've slept in just to
sleep next to you a little while
more.

i just wish i would have known when the last time was going to be the last time.

Selfish

I am a greedy lover.

I want you

only to myself.

(please don't leave me.)

Redamancy

If my tongue were a paintbrush,

I'd drag it across her frame,

starting from her neck,

down to her ankles,

stroking along

her every corner

and every curve,

just to prove

to her that

she is art.

Burning Bridges

I've become a master at burning the same bridges I wasted my time building.

Hookup

I'm your midnight text,
the dirty thoughts running through
your conscious when you're lonely
and attempting to forget.

I'm your favorite second option,
the lingering goosebumps on the
back of your neck.

I'm the filter at the
mouth of your cigarette, keeping
you safe, yet burnt away with threat.

I'm the shadow following
your footsteps,
a washed-away silhouette.

Fooling Myself

I'd be lying straight out of my teeth if I told you that I adjusted the collar of your shirt only because the ends were a little crooked.

I used that as an excuse just to be able to touch you again.

My hands have never been so familiar with a place than the bend of your neck.

Chronology

We met as strangers,
hopeless strangers,
unknowing of our future.

We made memories as lovers,
whimsical lovers,
living life in our present.

We ended as strangers,
mournful strangers,
forgetting what we shared
in our past.

Empty

A month after our breakup, we both found ourselves in the same
city that we fell in love in. You texted me, asking if you could take me
out for coffee. I knew I should have said no, but I missed you far too
much to miss out on seeing your face again.

We didn't go out for coffee. Instead, you met me at my place on
36th and 3rd. As the hours crept by us, and the city slowly began
to light up, we passed our time answering each other's questions
with questions, and covering our faces with the ends of our sleeves
to disguise the tears.

You stayed over. You already missed your train back home
and the only place you could rest your tired head was on
the pillow next to mine. We slept next to each other that night.
Not a touch, not a sound, not a good-night kiss.

That night I dreamt of what it'd be like if we started from the
beginning, sharing a life with one another rid of remorse and
fabrication.

That next morning,
I woke up to an empty bed.

Fool

He told me he fears
commitment, but the
27 tattoos across his body
convinced me otherwise.

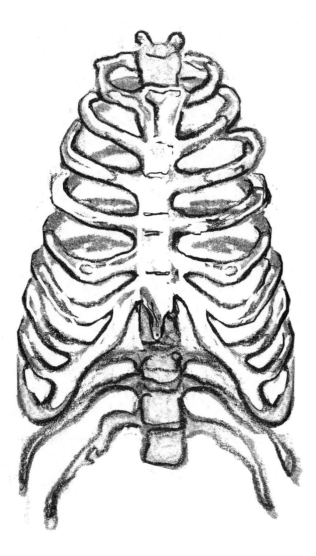

be still my dear,
　　let your body melt into mine.

may your ribs collide within my lungs until we can no longer breathe the
same air. i long to feel the warmth of your tongue run down my naked hips
as you take complete control of the flow of oxygen escaping my neck.

pull the hair from my scalp
　　as i tear the skin off your back

take a bite from my lips
　　and let my words trickle down the sides of your mouth.

allow me to crawl inside your corpse and play a tender hymn
with the keys growing along your spine.

　dig your snaggle teeth around my heart so you can taste what has left me
so bitter.

you'll take blood from underneath and wear it as war paint across your face,
　　for my vessel was once a war-zone tattered by jaded lovers.

　　and i'll drink the tears from your eyes
　　　　as i burn memories of us into the back of my mind.

i crave nothing more than to become one with you.

July 19, 2016

~~[scribbled out]~~

~~[scribbled out]~~

~~[scribbled out]~~

THIS TIME LAST YEAR ~~[scribbled out]~~ TOLD ME THAT HE LOVED ME FOR THE FIRST TIME. THIS TIME LAST YEAR I CRIED TEARS ~~[scribbled out]~~ LEAVING HIS HOUSE BECAUSE I HEARD THOSE WORDS.

~~[scribbled out]~~

THOSE

THREE

WORDS.

THIS TIME LAST YEAR I MEANT SOMETHING MORE THAN A ONE SIDED FLING TO SOMEONE.

THIS. TIME. 365. DAYS. AGO.

HE DOESN'T TALK TO ME ANYMORE.

I THINK HE'S ALREADY FORGOTTEN ABOUT THIS TIME   LAST   YEAR.

i gave him the moon and stars. but all he wants is space.

Wildflowers

What started as a solitary rose swiftly turned
into an untamable garden.

You grew wildflowers in my body, and since you left,
I've been attempting to pick out the thorns.

It began as pure innocence, but now the stems wrap tightly
around my lungs, making it hard to breathe.

Like a seed, you are planted in me—

Don't you remember?

Hindsight

I told myself that you would never make it into the pages of this book.

That was far before I knew you'd ever be the one to break my heart.

The Fixing

What we shared was a tender and woeful curiosity—

Nothing more than a brief dalliance fabricated with the belief that
our brokenness could heal one another.

4:15 a.m.

You
are
spiritually
broken—

you
became
the
person
who
hurt
you.

—and you eventually went back to her too.

à toi, pour toujours.

x

Hold On

Truth be told, I was never yours. No matter how hard I tried convincing myself that I was, or could be, nothing could make me stop you from wanting her.

We had our good days.

Like the evening we spent together taking a stroll along the Santa Monica Pier in the midst of the California chaos. We watched the children run along the edge, cotton candy in hand, as their mothers chased uncontrollably after them. You bought me a flower from a local peddler and observed my every move as I picked its petals off, one by one, and tossed them carelessly into the Pacific coast.

With our good days came our bad ones.

Like the morning you flew to New York City to see her in the midst of my trip visiting you in Los Angeles, leaving me alone in a city I was far too unfamiliar with. You took the first flight across the country and didn't even tell me until you were already gone. I picked up my first cigarette that night because of you. I thought that maybe it would make me feel something because I would watch you from afar inhaling tobacco like therapy. Yet, at no chance was anything able to ease the pain you put me through.

I fucking hate smoking.

You were always mine, but I was never yours.

And tomorrow we will remain the exact same—

I'll still be here placing together the remaining pieces you refused to finish.

Fault

I built
the ship
that sailed
her away.

Manipulation

You ripped apart my petals,
one by one,
as if we were playing
a childlike game.

he loves me
he loves me not
he loves me
he loves me not
he loves me
he loves me
not

You played me often,
seeing if I would stay
or if I would leave.
If you could hold me
in your grip tighter
or if I'd be better off
wilted on the soil that
helped me grow.

he loves me
he loves me not
he loves me
he loves me not
he loves me
he loves me
not

I'll never understand
what gave you fulfillment
in picking apart the pieces of me
that you claimed to love so dearly.

he loves me
he loves me not
he loves me
he loves me not
he loves me
he loves me
not

With every blade you
threw to the ground,
you got closer to my roots
and conceived a realization
of who you made me out to be.

he loves me
he loves me not
he loves me
he loves me not
he loves me
he loves me
not

You grew fond of my pretty
but never my essence,
and there wasn't a single thing
that I could do except sit back
and watch you steal the parts of me
I was still learning how to love.

he loves me
he loves me not
he loves me
he loves me not
he loves me
he loves me

not

Not Yours, Never Was

Like the ocean, you only knew how to love in waves.

You failed to recognize that I am the rocks upon shore that kept
grounded and would carry you in whenever you longed for more.
I watched you stay and I watched you leave, resting gentle kisses on
my flushed cheeks as if it meant something to you.

What a strange feeling it is to lie next to someone you hold so closely
to your heart yet still feel so alone.

*—that's when reality settled in the air between us and suddenly
it was all beginning to feel one sided again.*

A Rose

I was too busy
admiring the petals
that I forgot
about the thorns.

—*seeing nothing but the good in others is both a blessing and a curse.*

you are your home.

Radio Silence

Your disregard

toward me

was never

empty;

it was

always

full of

answers.

Sad Lovers

You know, I wonder if there will ever be a time where it doesn't hurt
to talk about it. The doors slamming, the hair pulling, the arguing
back and forth until our lungs grew cold. My "yes" and your "no." My
"stay'" and your "go." You leaving, as I stuck behind in that desolated
room on your splintered floorboards. I wonder if there will ever be
a time in my life when I can spit out your name without feeling the
desire to sink my teeth deep within the sides of my mouth. To talk
about how effortless it was for you to walk away without tasting the
warm and bitter aftertaste of you letting go. See, for you, this was
just another thing to place on that shelf of yours. That shelf that
holds all of your woes you refused to touch in fear of making yourself
appear weak.

I've howled at my reflection until I couldn't recognize myself
anymore. My hands and knees are bruised through every layer of
flesh just from crawling beneath your expectations. You will never
change. You will never change. You will never change. I just don't
understand what convinced me to believe that you were capable of
doing so. I couldn't fix you. God, did I try.

Sad people just can't fix sad people.

Spanish Guitar

The moonlight leaked through your window shutters
and I wore its light across my breasts like silky lingerie.

I watched your eyes meet mine
through the darkness in your living room
as you observed my every edge and curve.

I felt your cold hard gaze grace upon me
as a blanket of chills waltzed across my bare skin.

"Your body is shaped like a Spanish guitar."

"Why, thank you. Now come over here and play me."

Looking Back

I loved you
in ways
I never even
loved myself.

Dream On

Infatuated with my own desirable imagination,
I turned myself into a victim of my own romanticization.

every woman who comes after

will see me deeply bedded inside of you.

A Confession

As much as I won't let myself admit it, I think I was just as terrified as you were. Everything that I felt when I was with you was foreign; it felt so real that it scared the fuck out of me. I've been in relationships before, serious ones in fact, but I swear, every time you said my name, those butterflies that were once there turned into time bombs just waiting to explode. I lost countless nights of sleep just thinking about you.

The first time I slept over at your place, I consumed most of those hours staring blankly at you, studying your body, trying to detect one single flaw. I spent a lot of time nodding in agreement to what you were saying, but if I'm being frank, I wasn't listening to a goddamn thing that was leaving your mouth that night. I was more fixated on attempting to reveal a single thing, anything really, wrong with you, but I couldn't. Everything about you was everything I could ever want and more. I then began trying to assure myself that love is blind and it's only a matter of time before the whole "lust" thing would wear off, but time became my enemy because the more of it I spent with you, in your company, the harder I fell in love.

I knew you'd break my heart. I could see it in your eyes; they never fail to lie. Even then, that didn't stop me from offering all that I have to you because you were the one, I swear to God, you were the only one.

I believe that you loved me too. I think when you slowly began to realize how real we had it, it all set in and that's when you decided to run away. To just cut the cord quick and pretend like it never happened in the first place before we got any further.

I used to blame you for the pain that you left me with, but I'm not quite sure I do anymore. Seeking closure for far too long made me pinpoint the fear that very much lived inside of me too. We are young, so fucking young, and I truly and earnestly believe that you and I met at the wrong time.

I believe that somewhere there is another world waiting for you and me. Maybe, one day, when we're older, we will meet once more and things will be different for us. That when we look into each other's eyes after years and years of being apart, it will all make sense. That you will see the 18-year-old naive girl in me who fell madly in love with you and wouldn't give you up for the entire universe.

Maybe one day, we'll meet again and that's when you'll recognize that it was always us. And you'll read these words and think of me.

And when you do, I'll be right here beside you.

Flux

I miss the little things.

Like the nights we would dress up and I could feel the slight touch of your knuckles trailing up my spine as you zipped the back of my dress. Or the early mornings we would force ourselves to get out of bed just to dance to jazz in the kitchen and make blueberry pancakes. I miss watching you fall asleep slowly and then all at once as I tried syncing my every breath with yours. I miss the sound of your fingertips attempting to strum a melody out of your roommate's guitar and laughing when you realized that it was out of tune. I miss making you late for work because I just wanted one more kiss. Or two. Or five.

I miss you poking at the way I'd mispronounce a word and how you'd kindly correct me afterward. I miss accidentally falling asleep while watching a film and arguing with you that I was awake the entire time when we both knew well enough that I wasn't. I miss looking at you and knowing exactly what you were thinking. But ultimately, what I miss the most is the person you were when I first met you. I understand that we are growing up as humans must and that change is inevitable, but goddamn, if I knew you'd become the person you promised you'd never be, I don't think I'd be missing you anymore.

Missed Connection

I hung up the phone
before you stuttered
out the words

"i love you"

so I wouldn't
feel guilty
when I would
have to say it back.

Melancholy

Because for once,
my words weren't just used
to fill a void between
the silence in our sheets,

but also as a mantra
to remind myself that
I am loved.

Even if you
aren't
the one telling
me.

Acknowledgments

First and foremost, I'd like to thank my marvelous manager, Rana Zand, and attorney, Jessica Marlow. Without the help of their patience and wise decisions, this book wouldn't be in your hands today. Massive thank-you to my unbelievably talented illustrator, Katie Roberts, for turning my words into art. Her visuals truly brought my poetry to life—something I've always dreamt of one day seeing. Along with that, thank you deeply to Emily Ann for being the mastermind of *Flux*'s cover. I wanted nothing more than to have a team of badass ladies by my side to help me bring this piece of soul to life, and I couldn't be any more fortunate to have had the help of their brilliant minds.

Thank you to my dearest friends and beautiful sisters, who have been there for me every single brutal step of the way. From being shoulders to cry on, people who consoled me, excellent advice givers, and staying up with me until sunrise reading my words—you all are the reason I faced my fear of sharing my poetry with the world. Thank you for being with me when I needed you all the very most.

Mom and Dad, your nurture and endearment for me are what grew me into the woman I've become today. Despite the issues I've faced growing up, you both have never failed to make me feel important. Thank you for teaching me how to love with every single bone in my body.

A special thank-you to Andrews McMeel and Patty Rice for believing in my words. Also thanks for making me cry while I was working my shitty retail job that day I received an email that you all wanted to publish my book. I will never forget that life-changing afternoon.

To the ones who broke my heart, thank you for once loving me. What was once a magical bond between two people has turned into a righteous, unbreakable self-love like no other.

The pain I dealt with was by leaps and bounds the most difficult thing I've ever had to mourn through, but the lessons learned in the end made it all worth it. Thank you for teaching me how to be a better lover and an even better writer. If you're reading these words and it brought back any sort of memories, just remember that they're there forever. I live inside of you, whether you like it or not.

My many thanks to my kind, supportive, and delightfully dearest readers. Thank you for trusting me enough to have even made it to this page. From the very beginning, you all have held me together. Without the mammoth amount of love and support I've received, I don't believe I would have worked so hard to create this. My love and gratitude are with you all until the end of time.

Last, but not least, to 7-year-old me. You finally did it. You wrote your first book.

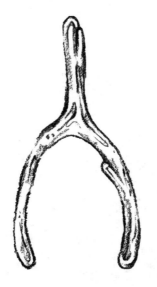

Index

Orion Carloto is a writer, poet, and influencer born and raised in a small town in Georgia. Popularly known on YouTube, Orion has sought to create a visual dreamworld for the lovers, the dreamers, and the brokenhearted. Growing up with her nose rooted in a book and deep in her own imagination, it came as no surprise that she wanted to write a book of her very own one day. Pulling inspiration from her personal adventures growing up, being in love, battling mental health, and the brutal pain of losing it all, she dug deep in her own woes and allowed those sorrows to fuel her writing. Orion now lives in New York with her feline lovers, Atticus and Lolita, and enjoys collecting mugs, baking sweets, sipping hot coffee, shooting with her vintage film camera, and watching French films.

Visit OrionCarloto.com.

Andrews McMeel Publishing
a division of Andrews McMeel Universal
1130 Walnut Street, Kansas City, Missouri 64106

www.andrewsmcmeel.com

17 18 19 20 21 BVG 10 9 8 7 6 5 4 3

ISBN: 978-1-4494-8932-8

Library of Congress Control Number: 2017941973

Editor: Patty Rice
Art Director: Holly Swayne
Production Editor: Mariah Marsden
Production Manager: Cliff Koehler

attention: schools and businesses
Andrews McMeel books are available at quantity discounts with bulk purchase
for educational, business, or sales promotional use. For information, please e-mail
the Andrews McMeel Publishing Special Sales Department:
specialsales@amuniversal.com